How Artists Use
Pattern and
Texture

REVISED AND UPDATED

PAUL FLUX

Heinemann
LIBRARY

www.heinemann.co.uk/library
Visit our website to find out more information about Heinemann Library books.

To order:
☎ Phone 44 (0) 1865 888066
🖷 Send a fax to 44 (0) 1865 314091
🖳 Visit the Heinemann Bookshop at www.heinemann.co.uk/library to browse our catalogue and order online.

First published in Great Britain by Heinemann Library, Halley Court, Jordan Hill, Oxford OX2 8EJ, part of Harcourt Education. Heinemann is a registered trademark of Harcourt Education Ltd.

Editorial: Clare Lewis
Design: Joanna Hinton-Malivoire
Picture research: Melissa Allison
Illustrations by Jo Brooker/Ann Miller
Production: Julie Carter

Printed and bound in China by South China Printing Co. Ltd.

13-digit ISBN 978 0 431 16214 0
11 10 09 08 07
10 9 8 7 6 5 4 3 2 1

British Library Cataloguing in Publication Data
Flux, Paul
How Artists Use: Pattern and Texture.
745.4

Acknowledgements
The publishers would like to thank the following for permission to reproduce photographs:
AKG, London: pp. **16**, **24**; Boomalli Aboriginal Artists, Purchased with the assistance of funds from National Gallery admission charges and commissioned in 1987. Collection: National Gallery of Australia, Canberra: p. **12**; Bridgeman Art Library: Arts Council Collection, Hayward Gallery, London p. **21**, Alan Bowness Hepworth Estate / Bristol City Museum and Art Gallery p. **18**, British Library, London p. **27**, Christie's Images / Private Collection / © ARS, NY and DACS, London 2006 p. **9**, Scottish National Gallery of Modern Art, Edinburgh / © ADAGP, Paris and DACS, London 2006 p. **19**, State Russian Museum, St. Petersburg p. **13**; Trevor Clifford: p. **23**; Corbis: Richard Hamilton Smith p. **7** bottom left, © ADAGP, Paris and DACS, London 2006 p. **20**, Bojan Brecelj p. **5**, Angelo Hornak p. **11**, Matthew McKee, Eye Ubiquitous p. **15**; M.C. Escher's "Metamorphosis 11" c.2000, Cordon Art B.V.-Baarn-Holland. All rights reserved. p. **22**; Hunterian Art Gallery, University of Glasgow, Mackintosh Collection: p. **10**; Oxford Scientific Films: pp. **6**, **8**; Photodisc: p. **7** top left and bottom right; SCALA: p. **28**; V & A Picture Library: p. **26**; Werner Forman Archive: pp. **4**, **17**; Woburn Abbey; p. **14**.
Cover photograph of *Unititled (screenprint)* by Victor Vasarely reproduced with permission of © ADAGP, Paris and DACS, London 2006. Photo: The Bridgeman Art Library/Private Collection.

Contents

Any words appearing in the text in bold, **like this**, are explained in the Glossary.

What is a pattern?

A pattern is a shape or **design** which is **repeated**. If you draw a simple shape, colour it, and repeat it, you start to build a pattern. Patterns can be simple or complicated. Artists have used pattern for thousands of years, both to **decorate** and to add meaning to their work. Here you can see a **mosaic** from a palace in Spain – not all patterns are as complex as this one though!

Mosaic, Alcazar of Seville, 14th century

Chinatown, New York

In the modern world patterns are everywhere. It is sometimes hard to see them all because there are so many. How many patterns can you find in this picture? The signs, the shapes of the buildings, and the vehicles all mix together to make a mass of pattern and colour. You can almost hear the noise! How dull everything would be without pattern.

Patterns and texture

Nature loves using pattern! We are surrounded by the most complicated and beautiful **designs**. Pattern can change how we see something. Plants can look like stones, insects can look like leaves! Nature makes wonderful patterns everywhere you look. Could you make patterns like these?

stick insect

germander speedwell flower

butterfly fish

stone flower

What do you think the surface of the things on these two pages would feel like? Would they be rough or smooth, soft or hard, dry or slippery? The way the surface of an object feels is called its **texture**. Many artists try to show how things in their pictures would feel if you could really touch them.

garter snake

tarantula

swallowtail butterfly

Unusual patterns: nature in art

Wind and rain can wear rocks away at different rates. When this happens the effect is sometimes **dramatic**. Sandstone rocks can make particularly colourful patterns in the changing light of day. These patterns have been cut over thousands of years and are still changing today. Do they look as if they are moving? How do you think these rocks would feel?

Rock formation, Colorado, USA

Georgia O'Keeffe, *Out Back of Marie's*, 1930

Have you ever seen hills and mountains look like this? Georgia O'Keeffe has painted a **landscape** in which the folds of the rocks seem to be moving. It is as if the land is alive. The colours, **textures**, and patterns the artist used can all be found in nature, but she has mixed them together in her own way.

Artists' patterns

Charles Rennie Mackintosh, *Wave Pattern: Green, Purple, Pink, Orange and Black*, 1915–23

Charles Mackintosh was a Scottish **architect** and designer. He made this **design** to be printed on cloth more than 80 years ago. The patterns move from side to side, and also up and down. Notice how the artist has used a grid to help him make the pattern. Everywhere you look you can see shape, colour, and line being **repeated** in this unusual design.

Chimneys, Hampton Court Palace, London, about 1520

Patterns and **textures** can be found in the most unlikely of places! This group of chimneys is at Hampton Court Palace, near London. The palace was built nearly 500 years ago, when open fires were the only way of heating a building. The palace has dozens of chimneys and each one is different! Why don't you design a chimney pattern yourself?

Shapes make patterns

Do you recognize the shape that is **repeated** here? It is the **continent** of Australia painted in bright, exciting colours. In between these shapes are more traditional **Aboriginal designs**. The two parts of the pattern are very different from one another, but they do not clash. Can you see how the dotted black and white lines are used to make space in the picture?

Jeffrey Samuels, *This Changing Continent of Australia*, 1984

Pavel Filonov,
Faces, 1940

Pavel Filonov was a Russian artist who began painting around 100 years ago. In this picture patterns swirl and **collide**, and suddenly faces can be seen. How many can you find? You should see three. The faces slowly appear from under the patterns and the eyes look straight at you. They seem trapped beneath the ever-moving shapes.

Patterns with meaning

Pattern can help make the meaning of a painting clear. Here is a **portrait** of Queen Elizabeth I, painted after England defeated the **Spanish Armada** in 1588. The picture is full of symbols of her power: the crown, her hand on the globe, and the Armada sailing to destruction. But look also at her clothes! The fine pattern and **texture** of her dress tell us that this is a very powerful person who can afford expensive clothes, and an artist to paint her!

Artist unknown, *Elizabeth I Armada Portrait*, 1588

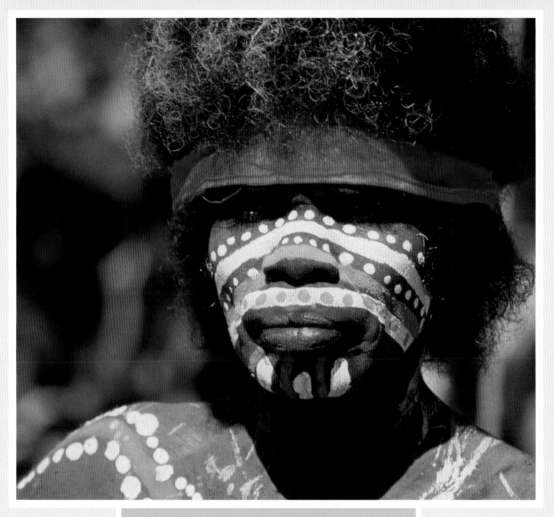

Aboriginal man with painted face

People have decorated their bodies for thousands of years. Often they do this to make themselves feel special in some way. This **Aboriginal** man has painted his face with stripes and dots. Perhaps he is about to take part in a ceremony. Have you ever had to get dressed up to do something special? How did you feel?

Patterns and texture in nature

Artists often try to copy the patterns they find in nature. Here the Austrian artist Gustav Klimt has painted a birch wood in autumn. He has looked very hard at the patterns, **texture**, and colour of the bark, and has copied the huge range he has seen. These patterns, textures, and colours make us realize just how beautiful some ordinary places can be, if we look hard enough.

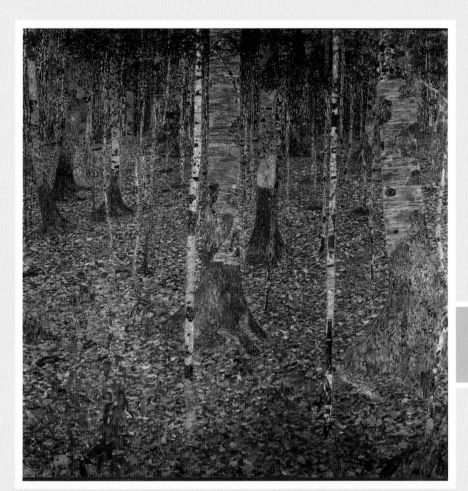

Gustav Klimt,
Birch Forest,
1903

Not all patterns that artists find in nature are complicated. Sometimes the simple ones work just as well. These flowers were painted on a screen in Japan, over 300 years ago. The **delicate** colours and shapes have been perfectly copied by the artist. The leaves, flowers, and stems are carefully arranged across the picture space. Does this picture make you feel calm and peaceful?

Pattern at work

Barbara Hepworth made this picture shortly after the end of World War II (1939–45). She had spent some time in a hospital and admired the work the **surgeons** did there. The five figures stand in a row, all looking the same way, perhaps at the patient. Three of the surgeons make a **repeated** pattern. They look similar, apart from the position of their hands.

Barbara Hepworth, *The Hands*, 1948

Fernand Léger,
*Constructors:
The Team at
Rest*, 1950

The French artist Fernand Léger painted this picture of men
putting up a metal frame for a new building. The strong
patterns and colours of the building frame support the
men at work and those resting. The men's hands are larger
than usual because the painting is about **physical** work. The
simple, repeated patterns in the building frame and the
men's clothes give the picture a tough feel.

Pattern on the move

In the 1960s, some artists became interested in the special effects that pattern and light can have on the eye. This sort of art is called **Op Art**, short for Optical Art. Line and shape **combine** to make this dazzling pattern. The pattern is the whole point of the painting, there is nothing else. Look at this for a while and the shapes can seem to move. How does this picture make you feel?

Jean Pierre Yvaral, *Untitled*, 1965

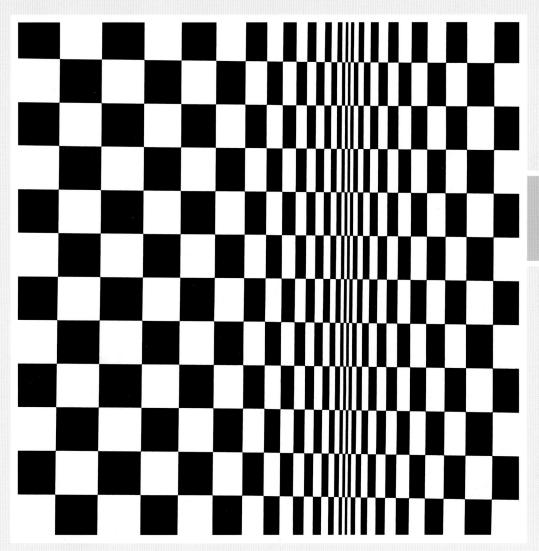

Another artist who became interested in Op Art was the British painter Bridget Riley. She sometimes used just shape and line with no colour, completing a number of pictures in black and white. Some are very difficult to look at for long, because they disturb the eyes so much. It can be difficult to realize that this picture is just a flat surface!

Patterns that fit together

Shapes that fit together with no spaces between them are said to **tessellate**. M. C. Escher, a Dutch artist, made many pictures with shapes that work together to make patterns. How many different patterns and shapes can you see in this very long picture? Look how they change into each other.

M.C. Escher, *Metamorphosis II*, about 1940

A jigsaw piece is a kind of tessellation and is really easy to draw.

Do it yourself!

1. Copy the jigsaw pieces here, or make up your own.
2. Inside the pieces draw patterns or a picture you like.
3. You could even stick the whole thing onto card and then cut it out to make a real jigsaw.

Pattern, colour, and shape

The Russian artist Kasimir Malevich painted this picture. He used simple shapes and only a few colours. We can see four faceless figures standing in line. Malevich wants to remind us of Russian religious paintings, which often show saints in a line across the picture. The half-white faces and patterned bodies make us wonder what the picture is about.

Kasimir Malevich, *The Athletes*, 1928–32

Do it yourself!

1. Copy the four figures below onto a piece of paper
2. Colour them with patterns of your own.
3. Don't use too many colours. Keep the patterns simple.
4. Colour part of the background as well.
5. Have you found that, like Malevich, you can put feeling into ordinary shapes using careful colouring?

Making pattern work for you

William Morris was an English artist who designed carpets, furniture, tiles, and **stained glass**. In this stained glass design, the woman is playing a musical instrument, probably a lute. Morris has **divided** the space around her to look like tiles. The **repeated** patterns of daisies and sunflowers **decorate** the background in a quietly graceful way.

William Morris, *Woman Playing a Lute*, about 1872–74

This is a page from a hand-painted book made more than 1,300 years ago. It is simpler than it looks. Look at the middle four squares (a detail is shown on the right). Can you see how the pattern fits together?

Do it yourself!

1. Draw some squares and try making your own designs. Keep these simple at first, and make sure the corners match.
2. Try putting a flower or plant in the centre.

Page from Lindisfarne Gospels, about AD 698

Patterns old and new

Some of the oldest surviving patterns were made by the ancient Egyptians. This is the **sarcophagus** of the pharaoh Tutankhamen, made more than 3,000 years ago. Red and blue glass has been **delicately** placed between lines of gold, to create a beautiful pattern. The Egyptians loved bright colours, and often surrounded their art with patterned frames.

Sarcophagus of Tutankhamen, Egypt, about 1323 BC

Do it yourself!

1. The next time you paint or draw a picture, put a patterned frame around it.
2. Copy some of the squares below, or design your own.
3. Use two or three different squares and repeat them
4. If you use only a few colours, perhaps two for each square, you will soon have a decoration just as good as the ancient Egyptians made!

Glossary

Aboriginal native person of Australia

architect person who designs buildings

collide to crash or bump into something

combine to mix together

continent large area of land – Australia, Africa, Europe, North America, South America, Asia, and the Antarctic are all continents

decorate to make something more pleasant or interesting to look at

delicate very fine, gentle

design lines and shapes which decorate a picture

divide to split into two or more parts

dramatic something which is surprising or exciting

landscape picture of natural and man-made scenery, for example fields, trees and houses

mosaic picture or pattern made with small coloured stones, glass or tiles

Op Art short for Optical Art. A kind of painting in which lines and colour make the eyes see something which is not real. For example, pictures appear to move.

physical to do with the body

portrait painting which shows what someone looks like

repeat to do something over and over again

sarcophagus coffin

Spanish Armada fleet of ships which sailed from Spain to invade England in 1588

stained glass pieces of coloured glass put together to make a picture

surgeon doctor who performs operations in a hospital

tessellate shapes which fit together with no spaces between them

texture the feel or look of something

More books to read

Connolly, Sean. *The Life and Work of: Paul Klee*. Oxford: Heinemann Library, 2006.

Hosack, Karen. *How Artists See: Nature*. Oxford: Heinemann Library, 2004

Index

Titles in the *How Artists Use* series include:

Hardback 978-0-431-16212-6

Hardback 978-0-431-16213-3

Hardback 978-0-431-16214-0

Hardback 978-0-431-16215-7

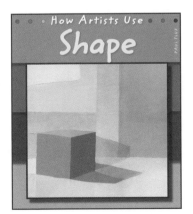

Hardback 978-0-431-16216-4

Find out about other titles from Heinemann Library on our website www.heinemann.co.uk/library